The VOICES
of Christmas

25 Messages of Hope

DREW SHERMAN · BO CHANCEY

The Voices of Christmas
Published by 41Press

For information or bulk sales:

41PRESS
Attn: Publishing Team
1308 Wellington Road
Manchester, NH 03104

publisher@41press.com

ISBN: 978-0-578-13072-9

Printed in China

CONTENTS

INTRODUCTION

What exactly is Christmas all about?

The period from Thanksgiving Day to Christmas is full of hype, grand expectations, and hopeful anticipation. Children are wide-eyed. Grown-ups hustle and bustle. The atmosphere is electric.

But why?

What is so special about this season we call Advent?

Christmas is a full sensory experience. There are wonderful sights, sounds, smells, tastes, and textures. There are wrapped packages full of hidden treasures, twinkling lights all aglow, voices ringing out joyful song, and delicious foods cooking in the kitchen. Families gather to celebrate. Churches are full of life. Christmas is on everyone's mind.

Many people share a growing concern over the commercialization of Christmas. There is a sense that the true meaning of this holy season is being lost amidst the whirlwind of activity, shopping, and pressure. Are the secular voices of consumerism, Santa Claus, and "Happy Holidays" drowning out the authentic voices of Christmas?

No…the sacred voices of Christmas cannot be silenced.

Christmas has always been and will always be about Jesus. The voice of God, the prophets, the scriptures, and the Church all testify to the truth of Christmas. Christ has come. God became flesh. Salvation is here.

We hope and pray that you and your family will hear clearly from God this Christmas. Enjoy His presence and add your voice to the Heavenly Host proclaiming that the greatest gift has come.

Merry Christmas,

Drew & Bo

December 1

The First
Voice

LISTEN

In the beginning God created the heavens and the earth. Now the earth was formless and empty, darkness was over the surface of the deep, and the Spirit of God was hovering over the waters.

And God said, "Let there be light," and there was light.

Genesis 1:1-3

In the beginning was the Word, and the Word was with God, and the Word was God. He was with God in the beginning. Through him all things were made; without him nothing was made that has been made. In him was life, and that life was the light of all mankind.

John 1:1-4

LEARN

Advent is the time of year that Christians expectantly wait and prepare to celebrate the birth of Jesus.

I encourage you to think about Christmas. Get into a Christmas frame of mind. What are your favorite Christmas songs, Christmas traditions, and Christmas foods?

Now picture Jesus. What do you see?

Thinking of Jesus during the Christmas season generally conjures up images of a baby wrapped in swaddling clothes. It is easy to imagine the infant Jesus lying in a manger with cattle lowing and shepherds dropping by unexpectedly to pay their respects.

Images of Christmas abound, but what about the voice of Christmas?

Have you ever wondered what Jesus' first words were?

It is fun to think about first words. I know that the first words that my children spoke were a really big deal to my wife and me. We both wanted them to say something different. She wanted them to say "momma" and I wanted them to say "da-da."

Our first-born had to deal with us constantly in her face trying to get her to say what we wanted. Then true to her free-spirited form, she did her own thing and said something completely different. Her first word revealed what she loved the most. She said "dog."

That is how goes with first words. They are often unexpected but totally revealing. My first word was "eat." That is not a shocker. To this day, I love food and think about it all the time. I finish breakfast and start daydreaming about lunch.

The first words of Jesus surprised me a bit. He did not say momma, da-da, dog, or eat. The first voice of Christmas was much more profound and revealing.

The first recorded words of Jesus were, "Let there be light."

The story of Jesus began way before His birth. Christmas did not begin with a baby in a manger. It began when the earth was formless and empty, when darkness was over the surface of the deep, and when the Spirit of God was hovering over the waters. The story of Jesus began in the beginning.

In the beginning, God spoke and it was.

Jesus is the Word. He is the Creator. In the beginning was the Word, and the Word was with God, and the Word was God. Jesus made everything.

Little Known Fact: The first recorded words of Jesus were "Let there be light."

Jesus is the life-giving force of creation. In Him was life and that life was the light of all mankind.

When the first voice said, "Let there be light," the revelation of Jesus began. Christmas is a continuation of the creation event as the Word became flesh and made His dwelling among us (John 1:14).

Jesus gives light to everything. Darkness retreats as He is revealed. The Christmas story continues as the first voice echoes in you. Jesus said, "Let there be light," and there was light. He declared to His followers, "You are the light of the world. A town on a hill cannot be hidden" (Matthew 5:14).

The first voice continues to ring out as Christ in you is revealed to the world. Do not muffle His voice this Christmas, and let there be light everywhere you go.

LIFT

Father, thank You for Advent and for the expectant joy that fills hearts this Christmas season. Help people to hear the first voice of Christmas as You continue to bring light to every dark corner of the world. Remind me that I am the light of the world because Jesus lives in me. Amen.

LIVE

Write a journal entry about how the first words of Jesus can be echoed in your life. Is there darkness in your life that needs to respond to His command to "let there be light"? How will Jesus use you as His light to bring life to others this Christmas?

JOURNAL

December 2

God with Us

LISTEN

Therefore the Lord himself will give you a sign: The virgin will be with child and will give birth to a son, and will call him Immanuel.

Isaiah 7:14

LEARN

A few years ago, I had the privilege of visiting the Holy Land with about 40 friends from our church. We saw some amazing sites. Among the most fascinating places we visited was the Israel Museum in Jerusalem. Trust me when I tell you that no visit to the Holy Land of Israel is complete without a visit to this incredible museum. Its four wings and expansive gardens provide a host of wonders around every turn. You can even view an ancient model of the city of Jerusalem which reconstructs the topography and architectural character of the city as it was prior to its destruction by the Romans in 66 A.D. Originally constructed on the grounds of Jerusalem's Holy Land Hotel, the model, which includes a replica of Herod's Temple, is now a permanent feature of the Museum's 20-acre campus. But the most incredible part of the Israel Museum is the Shrine of the Book. This is a white dome-like structure that houses the Dead Sea Scrolls, the oldest known biblical manuscripts in the world. The biblical treasures contained inside the Shrine of the Book are too numerous to mention, but its prize exhibit is the Great Isaiah Scroll which includes all 66 chapters of the Book of Isaiah. And our verse for today, Isaiah 7:14, might be the greatest of all of the verses in the book.

The voice of Isaiah first rang out in 735 B.C. Jerusalem was a thriving, growing city that was led by a king who came from the family tree of King David. His name was Ahaz. Now Ahaz was not a good king. He devoted himself to pagan worship and spent a lot of time building expensive, meaningless shrines, seeking the aid of every powerless religion he knew of. History tells us that he even sacrificed his own sons, burning them alive in a ritual to the idol Molech. So it's safe to say that Ahaz was not a king who was going to leave a positive legacy.

But Ahaz actually had a big part in the announcement of the very first Christmas. God said to Ahaz in Isaiah 7:10, "Ask the Lord your God for a sign." Pardon me, but I find that a bit humorous. God said, "Go ahead, Ahaz, ask me for a sign—I dare you!" And so here was his big chance to take part in prophetic history, and brilliant King Ahaz decided to act holy.

(I say "act" because that's precisely what it was.) Ahaz said, "I will not test the Lord thy God." In case you are wondering, God didn't like that answer. You can look it up in Isaiah 7:13. But all that really matters is what God said next to Ahaz:

"Therefore the Lord himself will give you a sign: The virgin will be with child and will give birth to a son, and will call him Immanuel." Isaiah 7:14

And so it was that God announced the birth of his Son to a man who never really paid attention.

I guess not much has changed over the years. God is still hoping that we will pay attention to Him. That's why He sent Jesus to rescue us.

Did you know that Immanuel or Emmanuel means "God with us"? Immanuel is the Hebrew form of the word, and Emmanuel is the Greek form of the word. Both spellings are correct and both mean "God with us." More importantly, they mean He longs to be near us. He announces new mercies every morning to each of us. He makes His grace available every day. He fervently watches our comings and our goings. He is a God of the people. And He loves to rescue us. He longs to be by your side.

> **Little Known Fact:**
> Immanuel is the Hebrew form of the word, and Emmanuel is the Greek form of the word. Both spellings are correct and both mean "God with us."

Oh, by the way, in case you are wondering what happened to Ahaz.

In recognition of his terrible leadership and its great cost to the nation, Ahaz was buried in a commoner's grave rather than the royal cemetery, never to be found again. But then again, almost 800 years later they buried another king from the line of David. They can't find His tomb either......

LIFT

Father, help me to remember that when You announced the birth of Your Son into this world, You did so with me in mind. You knew that I needed a Savior, and You were right. Thank You for sending Jesus to rescue me. I pray that You would open my eyes this Christmas that I might understand the true spirit of this sacred, holy day. Amen.

LIVE

God's gift of Jesus is the greatest Christmas gift of all. Write a Journal entry listing the blessings you have as a Christ follower. Describe how your life has changed now that Jesus is with you, by your side.

JOURNAL

December 3

LISTEN

For to us a child is born, to us a son is given, and the government will be on his shoulders. And he will be called Wonderful Counselor, Mighty God, Eternal Father, Prince of Peace.

Isaiah 9:6

Therefore God exalted him to the highest place and gave him the name that is above every name, that at the name of Jesus every knee should bow, in heaven and on earth and under the earth, and every tongue acknowledge that Jesus Christ is Lord, to the glory of God the Father.

Philippians 2:9-11

LEARN

Something magical happens in my house every Christmas morning. It is the one day out of the year when my children actually fight to serve one another. As we gather around the tree to open gifts, they all want to be the one who distributes the gifts to everyone else.

Watching them fight for the privilege of serving one another reminds me of the type of king that Jesus is. The Son of Man did not come to be served but to serve and to give His life as a ransom for many. Jesus is a king unlike any the world has ever known.

The voice of the prophet Isaiah tells us that we will call Jesus "Wonderful Counselor." This is a direct reference to Jesus' kingship. The Wonderful Counselor would rule His people with divine authority and everlasting love.

God's initial plan for His people was for them to be ruled directly by Him and not through any kind of earthly king. When the Israelites demanded a king like the other nations, they in essence rejected God's rule. God warned His people that their earthly kings would fail them. They would face oppression and injustice as kings exalted themselves above their people.

King after king brought heartache to the Israelites. There were 41 kings and one queen who ruled Israel, Judah, or both. They found themselves in constant struggle with famine, disease, and war. David was the Israelite king who most closely approximated the qualities of a godly king, but even his rule was riddled with wars, turmoil, and strife.

Thus the prophets and the people began to dream of a future king who would bring deliverance and restoration. They longed for a Wonderful Counselor who would lead them in a fashion their earthly kings had failed to exhibit. They hoped for a king who would possess a plan they could whole-heartedly put their trust in.

Seven hundred years before the very first Christmas, the prophet Isaiah announced the coming of a king unlike any the world had ever seen. This king would be called Wonderful Counselor. That particular designation was used to describe a king who would successfully implement and complete a marvelous plan of action. The Wonderful Counselor would be a king with a designated purpose.

God, in His infinite wisdom, had decided to send His own Son to become the only king the world would ever need. Jesus came into this world with a singular and grand purpose. Jesus came to save the world. The Wonderful Counselor came to carry out His perfect plan of redemption and salvation.

God's plan would forever change the world. Nations marvel at the plan of the Wonderful Counselor. The birth, life, death, and resurrection of Jesus have utterly changed the course of human history. His birth split time in two. His resurrection released us from the shackles of time completely.

Little Known Fact: 41 kings and 1 queen ruled Israel, Judah, or both.

In Jesus' final breath on the cross, He uttered these words, "It is finished."

The Wonderful Counselor's plan had come to completion in His death. Jesus came not to condemn the world, but to bring salvation. What a Wonderful Counselor indeed!

Is this a king you can serve? Is this a king you can follow? Is this a king you can obey?

One day every knee will bow and every tongue will confess that Christ Jesus is Lord. All will hail the king.

LIFT

Father, remind me today of Your wonderful plan of grace and forgiveness. As I prepare to celebrate Christmas, fix my eyes on Your plan of action. Protect me from the distractions that often come this time of year, and renew within me a sense of awe in what You have done. Use me to remind others that our primary reason for celebration is the revelation of You, our Wonderful Counselor. Let every part of my life hail Your Son Jesus as my King of Kings. Amen.

LIVE

Have you ever thought about what it would be like to be king? What would you do if you were a king? How do you think you would fail as a king? Write a journal entry about why Jesus is the perfect king and how your life can hail Him as such.

JOURNAL

December 4

Victory Cry

LISTEN

For to us a child is born, to us a son is given, and the government will be on his shoulders. And he will be called Wonderful Counselor, Mighty God, Eternal Father, Prince of Peace.

Isaiah 9:6

When he came near the place where the road goes down the Mount of Olives, the whole crowd of disciples began joyfully to praise God in loud voices for all the miracles they had seen: "Blessed is the king who comes in the name of the Lord!" "Peace in heaven and glory in the highest!" Some of the Pharisees in the crowd said to Jesus, "Teacher, rebuke your disciples!" "I tell you," he replied, "if they keep quiet, the stones will cry out." As he approached Jerusalem and saw the city, he wept over it.

Luke 19:37-41

LEARN

Although the scriptures say nothing about it, I am sure that the baby Jesus cried. After all, that's what babies do. They cry. They cry to let you know they are hungry, sleepy, or need to be changed. Babies cry because they depend on others.

At Christmas we remember that the Mighty God humbled Himself and became human. The fullness of God was clothed in the flesh of an infant. He was vulnerable as His power was wrapped in humility.

Most of us think that crying is an expression of weakness. Nobody wants to be called a crybaby, and we consistently teach our children to stop crying. Our attitudes toward tears could lead us to believe that the mighty never cry.

For instance, my dad is not the crying type. You won't see him boohooing in a movie or tearing up at every tender moment. No, my dad is old school. He is more of a man's man, and real men do not cry.

Or do they?

As a kid, I can remember two distinct times that my father allowed me to see him cry. The first was when one of his best friends was tragically killed in a plane crash, and the second was when our dog Ruff died. I will never forget the look on his face when I came home from school that day. With one look, I knew what had happened. When my mom came home, they sat and cried together. Ruff was an amazing dog!

Those two days are vividly etched in my memory but, not because they seemed out of character for my dad. In fact his crying seemed to be right in line with his character. Dad was never moved to tears because he was angry, afraid, or in pain. His were tears of love.

So it may seem a little strange to speak of the Mighty God crying, but I believe it fits perfectly with His character. Jesus cried because He loved much.

There are two times in the Bible that we know Jesus wept. The first is in John 11 at the tomb of Jesus' great friend Lazarus, and the second is in Luke 19 immediately following the triumphal entry when Jesus wept over Jerusalem. In both stories, it seems clear that Jesus' chief motivation was love, and there was about to be a great expression of victory.

In the case of Lazarus, Jesus then raised him from the dead. When He wept over Jerusalem, it was just one week before His resurrection. The two times Jesus cried were precursors to the greatest revelations of His mighty power.

Much more than just a baby born to a virgin, Jesus is the ultimate display of God's power on earth. Jesus was the fulfillment of every prophecy that declared "God is mighty to save." Jesus was the ultimate warrior king. He defeated every stronghold that would try to conquer the people of God. Ultimate victory and triumph are found only through the Mighty God, Jesus Christ.

On the cross Jesus cried out in a loud voice, "My God, my God, why have you forsaken me?" He breathed His last, and He stripped the forces of evil of all their power. Our Mighty

God has set us free from bondage and oppression. Nothing can rule or possess dominion over us except Him. The Mighty God reigns supreme because He conquered death and gives life to all who place their trust in Him.

This all began with a tiny baby in manger, but within that baby was the hope of all mankind. The Mighty God became a man to accomplish what we were powerless to do. He took our form so that He could remove our sin. Jesus' apparent frailty was the revelation of His greatest strength. Jesus made Himself nothing. He humbled Himself and became obedient to death, even death on a cross.

Christmas is a celebration of the Mighty God coming to us in a form that we can comprehend and trust. The celebration of His birth is a perfect reminder that our God is mighty to save. No matter who you are or what you have done, the Mighty God can bring victory to you today.

> ### Little Known Fact:
> There are two times in the Bible that we know Jesus wept, once outside of Lazarus' tomb and once over the city of Jerusalem.

LIFT

Mighty God, thank You for coming into this world in great humility to save me. Thank You for overcoming sin and for bringing victory into my life. Help me today to celebrate the victory that came through the birth of Jesus. Protect me from sin and fix my eyes on the true message of Christmas. You are mighty to save, and I praise You for rescuing me. Amen.

LIVE

Tears can reveal the depth and power of genuine emotion. God chose to reveal His true might through the great humility of a baby in a manger, tears of compassion, and the victory cry on the cross. Write a journal entry about how His might and victory can best be expressed in your life this Christmas.

JOURNAL

_____
_____
_____
_____
_____
_____
_____
_____
_____
_____
_____
_____
_____
_____
_____
_____
_____
_____
_____
_____
_____
_____
_____
_____
_____

December 5

LISTEN

For to us a child is born, to us a son is given, and the government will be on his shoulders. And he will be called Wonderful Counselor, Mighty God, Eternal Father, Prince of Peace.

Isaiah 9:6

On the day the LORD gave the Amorites over to Israel, Joshua said to the LORD in the presence of Israel: "Sun, stand still over Gibeon, and you, moon, over the Valley of Aijalon." So the sun stood still, and the moon stopped, till the nation avenged itself on its enemies, as it is written in the Book of Jashar. The sun stopped in the middle of the sky and delayed going down about a full day. There has never been a day like it before or since, a day when the LORD listened to a human being. Surely, the LORD was fighting for Israel!

Joshua 10:12-14

LEARN

Almost all organized sports have some version of the time-out. It is a way to get a break in the action, stop the clock from ticking, and regroup before proceeding with the game. Wouldn't it be great if life came with time-outs?

The hustle and bustle of Christmas often overwhelms, as there never seems to be enough time to get everything done. I bet that you would call a time-out at some point this Christmas if you could. A little break in the action and some extra time to regroup is often exactly what we need.

Calling a time-out does have biblical precedence. Joshua called the first time-out when He asked the Lord to make the sun stand still, and it delayed going down for a full day. God fought for Israel on that day, and He is willing to fight for you today.

Time can be a trippy subject. The past often haunts us, the present overwhelms us, and the future makes us anxious. As you prepare your heart for Christmas, is it possible that you could benefit from the perspective and change that a time-out can provide?

When Isaiah referred to the coming messiah as Eternal Father, he was making a profound statement. He did not merely mean to suggest that Jesus would have an eternal kingdom, although that is true. Isaiah was stating that Jesus is the creator of time. Jesus has complete control and dominion over time, and is not subject to the laws of time. As Eternal Father, His reign will know no end and will ultimately be universal.

As your mind is flooded this year with memories of Christmas past, remember that Jesus is Lord over your past. Where there is regret, Jesus offers forgiveness. Where there is sorrow, Jesus gives hope. Where there is longing, Jesus provides fulfillment. Jesus is Eternal Father, and your past belongs to Him.

Jesus is also Lord of the present. The pressures of Christmas can be crushing. There may not seem to be enough hours in the day to accomplish all that we think needs to be done. It does not please God when we make Christmas frantic and hectic. Jesus longs to provide us with the proper perspective for Christmas. Allow Him to show you what is truly important, and then order your life accordingly. Slow down your pace. Refrain from busyness. Find rest and peace this Christmas in the presence of your Eternal Father.

Little Known Fact: Joshua called the first time-out when He asked the Lord to make the sun stand still, and it delayed going down for a full day.

Anxiety often sets in when we think about what the future holds. Jesus is Lord over that as well. We do not need to fear the future. Jesus told us what He was going to do. He has gone to prepare a place for us where we will dwell with Him forever. The Everlasting Father is preparing our eternal home! What on this earth is really worth worrying about?

When we dwell in the reality of Jesus as Eternal Father, we find the true joy of Christmas. Time does not define or control us because we belong to the creator of time. When the demands of Christmas become too much, just call a time-out, and Jesus will give you all the time you need to do everything He wants you to do.

LIFT

God, I praise You for being my Eternal Father. Thank You that You are Lord of my past, present, and future. Remind me this Christmas that You are greater than my past. Help me to order my present in a way that pleases and honors You. Let me find peace and rest this Christmas. Enable me to trust You with my eternity, and deliver me from worries regarding the future. Remind me to call a time-out whenever I am overwhelmed, and allow me to enjoy Your peaceful presence. Amen.

LIVE

Life can easily get out of whack as the tyranny of the urgent overtakes things of eternal significance. Seek your Eternal Father, and ask Him to give you all the time you need to do everything He wants you to do. Write a journal entry that includes a list of your top ten priorities for this Christmas.

JOURNAL

December 6

LISTEN

For to us a child is born, to us a son is given, and the government will be on his shoulders. And he will be called Wonderful Counselor, Mighty God, Eternal Father, Prince of Peace. Of the increase of his government and peace there will be no end.

Isaiah 9:6-7

"Come now, let us reason together," says the LORD. "Though your sins are like scarlet, they shall be as white as snow; though they are red as crimson, they shall be like wool."

Isaiah 1:18

LEARN

Chances are that you will be offered "peace" from a variety of sources this Christmas. For instance, your mom might offer you a piece of pie. A family member might be willing to give you a piece of their mind. An angry motorist might offer you one half of a peace sign. And even if you are naughty, Santa will probably still deliver a piece of coal.

All of that is fine and dandy, but it is not the kind of peace we are looking for.

People often dream of having a white Christmas, but what I have always longed for is a peaceful Christmas. Each year, I dream of escaping the trappings and pressures of Christmas to find a truly peaceful holiday experience. Why does it seem so difficult to discover consistent peace during the Christmas season?

I always think that it will be different. I try to plan ahead. I get my shopping done in advance. I prepare myself for encounters with family. I think that my efforts will somehow provide the perfect peaceful Christmas, but something always goes wrong. My efforts fall short, and peace escapes me.

When Isaiah announced the coming of a king who would be called the Prince of Peace, he was proclaiming the arrival of a peace that would know no end. The birth of Jesus ushered in a new era of peace. This kind of peace is not the absence of conflict. Jesus was clear in His statements regarding conflict. We will face trouble in this world. Trouble, stress, and heartache will still come our way, but the kind of peace Jesus brings is a peace that transcends our circumstances.

The true peace of Jesus begins on the inside and then manifests outwardly. The Prince of Peace can transform your life by dealing with the true reason for your lack of peace…sin. We are incapable of dealing with the internal turmoil that results from our sin. God reasons with us and offers to make our sins as white as snow. When our hearts are right with God, there is freedom to experience His peace regardless of what life throws at us. Now that is the kind of white Christmas worth dreaming about.

In John 14:27, Jesus said, "Peace I leave with you; my peace I give you. I do not give to you as the world gives. Do not let your hearts be troubled and do not be afraid."

The Hebrew word for peace is Shalom. It is often used as a greeting to say both hello and goodbye. It means "may peace be on you." The peace that Jesus offers this Christmas is more than a peace that can be on you. It is a peace that can be in you. When Christ comes into your life, His peace takes over and makes all things new. His peace covers all your imperfections like a blanket of pure white snow.

Little Known Fact:
The Hebrew word for peace is Shalom. It is often used as a greeting to say both hello and goodbye.

If you are looking for a peaceful Christmas, it won't be found in a mountain hideaway or in months of fastidious preparation. A peaceful Christmas can only be discovered through submission to the Prince of Peace. His peace will reign regardless of how our Christmas plans unfold. Spend time this Christmas resting in the security of the perfect Prince of Peace.

LIFT

Father, give me the wisdom to know how to receive the perfect peace of my loving savior. I need You to deal with my sin and to give me peace that moves from the inside out. Give me opportunities this Christmas to share Your peace with others. Remind me each day that, even though my circumstances change, Your peace always remains. Thank You for being my perfect Prince of Peace. Amen.

LIVE

Think about any challenging circumstances you are facing this Christmas. How can having a peaceful heart change your reaction to difficulties? God offers to give you peace by making your sins as white as snow. Will you take Him up on His offer? Write a journal entry and confess any sin that is robbing you of the peace of Christ.

JOURNAL

December 7

The Call of the Wild

LISTEN

A voice of one calling: "In the wilderness prepare the way for the Lord; make straight in the desert a highway for our God. Every valley shall be raised up, every mountain and hill made low; the rough ground shall become level, the rugged places a plain. And the glory of the Lord will be revealed, and all people will see it together. For the mouth of the Lord has spoken."

Isaiah 40:3-5

LEARN

One of the most popular Christmas movies of all time is Christmas Vacation, the story of the Griswold family's yuletide holiday adventures. It's not for everybody, but many of the scenes are sidesplittingly funny. Even now, just thinking about it, I am smiling. One of the more enjoyable characters is Clark Griswold's crazy cousin Eddie (played by Randy Quaid). Cousin Eddie has a big heart, but is a little short in the brains department. Anyway, let me ask you a question? Do you have a crazy cousin? I'll bet the answer is yes. Almost everyone does. By the way, if you don't' have a crazy cousin, be afraid. It may mean that you are the crazy cousin in your family!

Another reason I love Jesus is that He was so human. Jesus had a crazy cousin too. Let me tell you, John the Baptist was a wild one. Matthew 3:4 says, "John's clothes were made of camel's hair, and he had a leather belt around his waist. His food was locusts and wild honey." Let's just say, he was not your garden-variety prophet. But he was one of the greatest men who ever lived. And I am not exaggerating. Jesus paid him this compliment in Matthew 11:11 when he says, "I tell you the truth: Among those born of women there has not risen anyone greater than John the Baptist." I'd say Jesus loved his famous cousin.

You should love him too. He was such a crucial part of the Christmas Story. And Isaiah's words from chapter 40, verse 3 is one of the most beautiful Old Testament verses ever penned. "A voice of one calling: In the wilderness prepare the way for the Lord; make straight in the desert a highway for our God." That verse gives me cold chills just reading it. The desert voice.

Calling us to be ready. Challenging us to repent. Bringing us closer to Jesus.

John the Baptist was a purpose-driven, spirit-filled, powerful preacher. When some thought that perhaps he was the Messiah, he didn't allow that claim for one second. He simply reassured the people that someone much greater than he would be coming. My favorite John the Baptist quote of all time is from John 3:30. Consider these words of humility. "He must become greater and greater, I must become less and less." (NLT)

This Christmas make that your prayer: That people would see more and more of Jesus in your life and less and less of you. That Jesus would be more visible and that you would be in the background. My prayer for you is that you become more like John the Baptist. This is one crazy cousin that you want to imitate.

Little Known Fact:
Jesus had a crazy
cousin too.

LIFT

Jesus, I pray that You would give me the wisdom and humility to be more like You today. My prayer is similar to the one who prepared the way for You. May they see more and more of You in my life and less and less of me. I want to be like You. Help me to love, lead, and live like You would want me to. And may You be glorified in my life. Amen.

LIVE

John the Baptist's sole purpose was to prepare the way for Jesus and to point people to the Lord. Write a journal entry and list three people you can invite to church this Christmas Season. Now pray that God would give you the words to say to these precious souls so that you can prepare the way for Jesus to do a good work in their lives.

JOURNAL

December 8

LISTEN

But you, Bethlehem Ephrathah, though you are small among the clans of Judah, out of you will come for me one who will be ruler over Israel, whose origins are from of old, from ancient times.

Micah 5:2

LEARN

I remember January 1985 like it was yesterday. That's when I left my hometown of Brazil, Indiana, never to reside there again. At the wise old age of 18, I was ready to leave that sleepy, little town. I was moving on to a bigger and better world, ready to put that place in my rear-view mirror. I vividly remember rolling down the window of my ugly maroon, 1978 Buick Skylark and yelling at the top of my lungs, "SO LONG, BRAZIL, SEE YOU ON THE FLIP SIDE!" And I remember zipping down Interstate 70 without a care in the world.

It's kind of weird in hindsight, talking to a town as though it can hear me. And then we read Micah 5:2. This is the voice of Micah, a messenger of the Old Testament who prophesied from 737-690 B.C. As you read the book of Micah, most of his prophecies are directed toward another town, the city of Jerusalem. But here, in chapter 5, he speaks to a much smaller city. And when Micah speaks, he speaks with the authority of God. In fact, it could be argued that God speaks for him.

And, his conversation is with Bethlehem, the ancient city of Ephrathah. Maybe the only thing you know about Bethlehem is from the famous Christmas song, "O Little Town of Bethlehem." But did you know that Bethlehem means "house of bread"? This is very compelling considering its most famous resident, Jesus, would later declare himself the "Bread of Life."

But, let's pause for a moment to wonder. Why speak to a town? Why this town?

Bethlehem was a city rich in Jewish heritage. I suppose its strongest claim was that it was home to King David's ancestors.

But seriously, of all places, why Bethlehem, a town of a few hundred people? Why not a place of geographical prominence? Why not a location of military power? Why not Rome? Why not Athens? Why not Alexandria?

What about Jerusalem? It was just a stone's throw away. Why not the sacred city?

Bethlehem was a lot like my hometown. It was not very big, and it was not very famous.

But that all changed with one silent night.

For it was in Bethlehem that Jesus, your Savior and mine, was born.

The religious leaders of that time should have seen him coming.

Micah 5:2 says, "But you, Bethlehem Ephrathah, though you are small among the clans of Judah, out of you will come for me one who will be ruler over Israel, whose origins are from of old, from ancient times."

Little Known Fact: Bethlehem means "house of bread."

Allow me to paraphrase: "Out of you, Bethlehem, this little spot on the road, will come someone very famous, someone they will tell stories about for generations and generations."

That's the beauty of Christmas. God used this little spot on the map to bring His one and only Son into this great big world.

Looking back, I admit I love my hometown. I spent so many wonderful Christmas seasons in my Indiana home. It was there that I lived out my childhood years. It was there that I named Jesus as my Lord and Savior. It was there that I met my beautiful wife. And that makes it a very special place in my heart. A very special town. My Christmas town.

Kind of like Bethlehem.

LIFT

Lord, thank You for small towns and for the simple things in life. Growing up, I never realized how special my hometown really was. It makes me feel good that You used insignificant people, places, and things to usher in the coming of Your precious Son to save me from my sins. This Christmas, will You use me to lead someone closer to You? I am ready, willing, and able to navigate someone Your way. I love You, Lord. Amen.

LIVE

Maybe as you read these words you feel a bit insignificant. Consider yourself lucky. God may just be waiting to use you in a very significant way. Will you be available to his leading? Remember, God loves to use simple things in order to advance His Kingdom. Write a journal entry describing how you will let God use you this Christmas season.

JOURNAL

December 9

Speechless

LISTEN

Then an angel of the Lord appeared to him, standing at the right side of the altar of incense. When Zechariah saw him, he was startled and was gripped with fear. But the angel said to him: "Do not be afraid, Zechariah; your prayer has been heard. Your wife Elizabeth will bear you a son, and you are to call him John. He will be a joy and delight to you, and many will rejoice because of his birth, for he will be great in the sight of the Lord. He is never to take wine or other fermented drink, and he will be filled with the Holy Spirit even before he is born. He will bring back many of the people of Israel to the Lord their God. And he will go on before the Lord, in the spirit and power of Elijah, to turn the hearts of the parents to their children and the disobedient to the wisdom of the righteous—to make ready a people prepared for the Lord."

Luke 1:11-17

LEARN

The Parents of John the Baptist were an integral part of the Christmas Story. Zechariah was a priest, and he loved his wife very much. Her name was Elizabeth. Together they lived honorably before God, careful in keeping His commandments and enjoying a clear conscience before God. They were very godly people. But there was a certain emptiness in their lives. They were not able to have children, and they were very old.

Does this story remind you of another couple in the Bible? You might remember that Abraham and Sarah were going through similar hardships. They longed to be parents. They prayed without ceasing. And their prayers had gone unanswered. Just when hope was all but lost, God gave them a son when they were at a very old age. Isaac was born. The same scenario is about to be played out, New Testament-style, with Zechariah and Elizabeth. Same song, second verse.

Now it's worth mentioning that not everyone in our society wants to be a parent. And I suppose that's probably best. Parenting is hard work. It requires a lot of time, attention and sacrificial love. I've always found it strange that people have to take a test and acquire a license to drive an automobile, but anyone can be a parent with no pre-qualifications. Parenting is a great privilege and a real joy. The end always seems to justify the means.

I know many infertile couples who desperately long to have children. They are prepared, both financially and emotionally, to be great parents. But for whatever reason, nature does not cooperate. Some opt for adoption, a very noble undertaking.

64

Still others accept their plight and choose to use their gifts to build the Kingdom of God. That was the case with Elizabeth and Zechariah. They were a couple totally devoted to God. Their dream of having children was a faded memory. And then God did the impossible. The angel Gabriel appears to Zechariah and announces that Elizabeth would have a baby boy. The son's name was to be John. John would bring joy for many years to Zechariah and Elizabeth and would be "great in the sight of the Lord" and instrumental in bringing God's people back to the Lord. But most of all, their son John would be the voice who would point the people to Jesus Christ, the Messiah. What an unbelievable honor!

Can you imagine hearing news like that? Scripture tells us that old Zechariah had a little issue comprehending the angelic announcement. So to teach him a lesson concerning his unbelief, Zechariah was struck speechless until the birth of the baby. Despite that minor setback, I suppose nothing could have kept Zechariah from the joy and awe of becoming the father of John the Baptist.

The births of our three children were three of the greatest days of my life. It was, and still is, a tremendous honor to be their father. Seeing them find success in academics, athletics, and social settings is a rewarding experience. But none of those achievements can match the joy of watching my children honor the Lord. Knowing that they have the grace and mercy of Jesus Christ on their lives is all the fulfillment that I'll ever need as a parent.

My prayer for you this Christmas season is that you will cherish your children for who they are and that you will take a moment and read them the story of Zechariah and Elizabeth and tell them how much you love being their parent. If you're children are grown, call them up and tell them what a blessing it has been to be their parent. Their reaction might render you speechless, too.

Little Known Fact:
Zechariah was struck speechless until the birth of the baby.

LIFT

Lord thank You for the precious gift of being a parent. Please help me to never take my role for granted. I ask You to bless my children this Christmas season. May they continue to understand how much You love them and care for them. Like you did for John the Baptist, please help them to have a heart for Your Kingdom and to use their gifts to point people to Your Son. Amen.

LIVE

Read Psalm 127 and journal your thoughts on the blessings of parenting.

JOURNAL

December 10

Good News,
Bad News

LISTEN

The angel went to her and said, "Greetings, you who are highly favored! The Lord is with you."

Luke 1:28

But the angel said to her, "Do not be afraid, Mary, you have found favor with God. You will be with child and give birth to a son, and you are to give him the name Jesus. He will be great and will be called the Son of the most High. The Lord God will give him the throne of his father David, and he will reign over the house of Jacob forever; his kingdom will never end."

Luke 1:30-33

For nothing is impossible with God.

Luke 1:37

LEARN

Christmas is often filled with good news/bad news scenarios.

Here are a few examples.

Good News: Your extended family will be coming into town for Christmas.

Bad News: They are all staying at your house.

Good News: "Dad, I bought you that new watch you really wanted."

Bad News: "And I paid for it with your credit card."

Good News: There are freshly-baked Christmas cookies in the kitchen.

Bad News: You can put your skinny jeans away until spring.

The angel Gabriel is only mentioned four times in the Bible, but he is one of the most well-known angels because of his role in the Christmas story. He had an unbelievably difficult task. Can you imagine bringing the news that he brought to Mary?

On one hand, Gabriel was announcing the coming of the blessed Messiah. This was the greatest news ever to be proclaimed. Gabriel certainly understood the magnitude of the moment and must have shared in the excitement.

On the other hand, Gabriel had to appear to a young virgin who would likely be terrified and deeply troubled by the message he would deliver. God used Gabriel to delicately yet authoritatively unveil His plan to the mother of Jesus.

70

In Luke 1:28, Gabriel began his announcement with a greeting and proceeded to inform Mary that she was highly favored and that God was with her. In essence, the angel is letting Mary know that God had chosen her to do something spectacular and that God Himself would sustain her throughout the process. Normally we would think this would be some pretty exciting news, but Mary's response was perhaps more indicative of how we might respond.

The scriptures tell us that Mary was greatly troubled at Gabriel's words. The appearance of an angel out of thin air did not seem to cause her great alarm, but his words were another matter entirely. Now at this point all the angel had said was that "she was favored by God and that God was with her." What about that is so troubling? Don't you want to be chosen by God for something great?

The truth of the matter is that when God calls us He interrupts our plans and changes the course of our lives. It is troubling to be chosen by God. Mary had her life laid out before her. She would marry Joseph, have children, and live a quiet, simple life. But now things would change. What would God do with her? What might God do with you?

The next words out of the angel's mouth were very appropriate. He said, "Do not be afraid." Then Gabriel proceeded to deliver some terrifying news. The Virgin Mary would become pregnant, face public humiliation, endure possible rejection from her fiancé, and deal with a dizzying array of unanswered questions. Fear is the natural response to what is unknown. In much the same way, we become afraid when God calls us to serve Him. How will our lives change? What might we miss out on? Will we have to suffer?

Mary then asked the perfect question, "How can this be?" We wonder the same thing when God chooses us. How could God possibly use me? Gabriel's answer was perfect. The angel said, "With God all things are possible." God can use a young virgin, and He can use you.

God calls us to do great things for Him. It is good news to be chosen by God, but there are always troubling elements to doing His will. Remember that the good always outweighs the bad, and the reward is always worth the cost.

You too are highly favored. Do not be afraid, for with God nothing is impossible.

Little Known Fact: The angel Gabriel is only mentioned four times in the Bible, twice in Daniel and twice in Luke.

LIFT

Father, thank You for choosing ordinary people to do extraordinary things. Thank You for calling me into Your service. Please calm my fears and allow me to hear Your voice clearly amidst the chaos of Christmas. Remind me that You are with me, that You are leading every step of the way, and that nothing is impossible for You. Give me courage to obey Your calling and to do the things You ask me to do. Help me carry out Your will this Christmas. Amen.

LIVE

Have you ever felt like God wanted to use you to do something, but you found yourself fearful of what it would entail? Write a journal entry about some good things God can do through you this Christmas. Identify your fears, and ask God to help you overcome them.

JOURNAL

December 11

The Voice of Reason

LISTEN

This is how the birth of Jesus the Messiah came about: His mother Mary was pledged to be married to Joseph, but before they came together, she was found to be pregnant through the Holy Spirit. Because Joseph her husband was faithful to the law, and yet did not want to expose her to public disgrace, he had in mind to divorce her quietly.

But after he had considered this, an angel of the Lord appeared to him in a dream and said, "Joseph son of David, do not be afraid to take Mary home as your wife, because what is conceived in her is from the Holy Spirit. She will give birth to a son, and you are to give him the name Jesus, because he will save his people from their sins."

Matthew 1:18-21

LEARN

I tend to be a bit impulsive at Christmas time. There is something about this time of year that causes me to throw caution to the wind and adopt a "just go for it" attitude. I will see a course of action and take it without much thought regarding the consequences.

It is important that I surround myself with people who can be the voice of reason. If I go shopping, I need someone to ask if it is really a wise purchase. If I take my kids sledding, I need someone to ask if the proper safety precautions have been taken. If I am enjoying a delicious Christmas treat, I need someone to remind me that one cookie instead of twelve is probably enough.

I always warn people that, if they are looking for me to be the voice of reason, we are all in big trouble.

My problem is that I make up my mind to do something without considering better alternatives. God has often provided people in my life to be the voice of reason. Listening to them has saved me untold amounts of grief and brought greater blessings into my life.

It is important to seek wise counsel when facing big decisions. There are times when a particular course of action seems completely appropriate, but God has other plans.

Joseph was faced with one of those decisions when an angel appeared to him in a dream as God's voice of reason. Joseph had just discovered that Mary was pregnant, and he knew beyond a shadow of a doubt that he was not the dad.

Mary was betrothed to Joseph. Betrothal is different from modern-day engagements. It was a legally-binding agreement that could only be broken by death or divorce. The betrothal period typically lasted twelve months, and during that time Mary and Joseph could have been referred to as being married, even though there had not yet been a ceremony or consummation.

Little Known Fact:
Betrothal is different from modern-day engagements. It was a legally-binding agreement that could only be broken by death or divorce.

Joseph had a real problem on his hands. He could not claim that the baby was his because that would be a lie, and it would have implicated him in breaking the betrothal customs. Divorcing Mary put her at risk because adultery could have been punished with death.

Joseph was an honorable man, and he wanted to do what was right, so he set his mind on what seemed to be an appropriate course of action. He planned to quietly end the betrothal and not expose Mary to public disgrace and risk.

God had a different plan, and He sent an angel with specific instructions for Joseph.

Joseph listened and did as the Lord instructed. He did not allow fear, impetuousness, or his first inclination to determine his reaction to the news that Mary was pregnant. The voice of reason prevailed, and God would later use the obedience of Joseph to protect the baby Jesus.

Take time this Christmas to seek God's will in everything. Listen to Him, and do as He instructs. God may use you in ways you never imagined possible.

LIFT

Father, help me to seek You in everything. Please pour out Your wisdom upon me and allow me to know Your will. I know that Your ways are higher than mine and that You have plans that I cannot fathom. Help me to overcome my fears and to faithfully obey. Amen.

LIVE

Think about a time in your life where you would have benefited from listening to a voice of reason. Write a journal entry about what you learned from the situation. Who does God use in your life to speak to you?

JOURNAL

December 12

LISTEN

And there were shepherds living out in the fields nearby, keeping watch over their flocks at night. An angel of the Lord appeared to them, and the glory of the Lord shone around them, and they were terrified. But the angel said to them, "Do not be afraid. I bring you good news that will cause great joy for all the people. Today in the town of David a Savior has been born to you; he is the Messiah, the Lord. This will be a sign to you: You will find a baby wrapped in cloths and lying in a manger."

Luke 2:8-12

LEARN

My wife and I very seldom quarrel. She is so easy to get along with, and after living 26 years together, we truly are the best of friends. But we do have an ongoing disagreement when it comes to nighttime TV. She always wants to watch the local news, and I always want to watch SportsCenter. Now before you call me shallow, consider my reasoning. The news depresses me. It's really the same old thing every night. Someone's house was a victim of arson. Someone took the life of another. A carjacking occurred on the west side. A child was abducted on the east side. I don't know about you, but I'm not looking for another reason to be depressed or anxious. Life seems to take care of that on its own.

Then there's the weather. We live in Texas. It's not a big mystery. "Tomorrow it will be sunny and hot, high around 98." I'll alert the media. Oh, wait! They are the media.

Sports are more cheerful. They're something everyone can rally around. Your favorite baseball team hitting home runs. Your favorite quarterback throwing touchdowns. Your favorite point guard sinking three pointers. That's news I can use. It's not all that important, but it's better than being depressed. Very rarely is good news ever reported on the evening news.

And now back to Christmas.

Picture a few lowly shepherds tending their sheep nearby. Suddenly an angel appears, and the glory of the Lord surrounds them like a shield. The Bible says that they were terrified. Scared to death. Did you know that about angels? In the Bible, angels are not sweet creatures who sit around on clouds and play harps.

And they honestly don't sing all that much. Most of them are simply messengers. They help God by helping us. Angels are more warriors for God than sweet creatures floating on clouds.

And this angel said, "Fear not, boys, I bring you good news of great joy which is for everybody. The Savior of the world was born today, and you are the first ones to hear of it."

Good news of great joy! Now that's something to be excited about. Not only that, but good news of great joy for all people. That's right! For everyone. Jesus came so that the whole world could one day experience life abundantly. His plan was simple. He would come down to our level, love on us, show His love and loyalty to the Father, and die on an old rugged cross.

As amazing as all of that seems, some 33 years later there would be another angel who would arrive unexpectedly boasting even better news. This angel was ushered down by a giant earthquake. He landed on top of the tomb of Jesus. It was the third day. And like the shepherds before them, the women that saw this angel were terrified. And the angel said, "Do not be afraid." Sound familiar? "Do not be afraid, for I know that you are looking for Jesus, who was crucified. He is not here, he is risen. Come see the place where he lay." Matthew 28: 5-6

Little Known Fact: Angels are not sweet creatures who sit around on clouds and play harps.

In that single, solitary moment, the angel declared the most incredible event in human history. Life as we know it has never been the same since. It's the best news these ears have ever heard. This Christmas, I pray that you will treasure the news that Christ was born. I also hope that you praise the Lord on High that He defeated the grave. That's news worth listening to.

It's way better than SportsCenter.

LIFT

Lord, thanks for bringing joy to my life today. That was some news I needed to hear. The fact that You sent Your one and only Son to live and die for me is the best news I could ever hope to hear. Thank You for changing the world and for giving me hope for tomorrow. Thank You, Jesus, You are the God of joy. You are the bringer of everything that is good, and I love You. Amen.

LIVE

Find the right moment today to tell someone some good news, perhaps through an encouraging word or words of affirmation. When you have done this, write a journal entry and describe how it felt to speak joy and encouragement into someone's life.

JOURNAL

December 13

The Host with the Most

LISTEN

Suddenly a great company of the heavenly host appeared with the angel, praising God and saying, "Glory to God in the highest, and on earth peace to men on whom his favor rests."
Luke 2:13-14

As God's fellow workers we urge you not to receive God's grace in vain. For he says, "In the time of my favor I heard you, and in the day of salvation I helped you." I tell you, now is the time of God's favor, now is the day of salvation.
2 Corinthians 6:1-2

LEARN

I often forget that Christmas is the world's biggest birthday party. It is first and foremost a day set aside to celebrate the birth of Jesus. We know this, but the meaning gets lost so easily amidst all of the trappings of modern holiday festivities.

If I'm not careful, I end up thinking that Christmas is all about me. That always leads to tremendous disappointment. Disappointment comes from gifts that I did not receive, by events that I was not invited to, and by family interactions that were less than stellar.

Christmas is far more satisfying when I focus on Jesus. I am free to enjoy the season when it is about Him and not about me. There is no pressure from misplaced expectations.

When I am honest about it, everything is more fun when it is not about me…even birthday parties. I have had birthday parties thrown in my honor, and the whole time, I just felt extremely uncomfortable. I kept thinking that being born isn't all that special. I mean everyone is born. It wasn't like I did any work in the birthing process. If anyone should have a party on my birthday, it should be my mom. After all, she did all the work.

I don't want a birthday party, but I do enjoy going to birthday parties. There is something magical about a well-planned birthday party. They often have festive themes and decorations. The games are fun. Watching the birthday boy or girl open gifts is always entertaining. And who doesn't love cake and ice cream?

One of the best things about a really great birthday party is that just when you think the fun is over…when you're saying your good-byes and thanking the host…you get handed a goody bag filled with party favors. Party favors are great because they are totally unexpected.

When I take my children to parties, I can hardly wait to get to the car to find out what is in their bags. There is always great anticipation as we dig through the bag and start playing with the inexpensive trinkets. The funny thing, though, is that those bags almost never make it from the car to the house. By the time we get home, the favors have lost their appeal and end up getting stuffed in a seat-back pocket or shoved under the front seat. Months later, while cleaning the car, I inevitably find a virtual graveyard of abandoned party favors.

Remember that Christmas is a birthday party. For Jesus' very first birthday celebration God invited shepherds to attend. There were no decorations. No games were played. The shepherds brought no gifts. Cake and ice cream were not served. It might not sound like much of a party except for the fact that God appointed the Heavenly Host to deliver the party favors.

For some reason, many people picture the Heavenly Host singing. The Bible does not say that they sang. That's probably a good thing because the singing is just about the worst part of every birthday party.

The Heavenly Host declared the Lord's favor on men and pronounced the gift of God's peace. Now that is a party favor worth keeping! As you celebrate the birth of Jesus this Christmas, think about the Lord's favor. God has granted you peace. He has given you the gift of life. What are you doing with God's favor? Are you experiencing it fully, or have you carelessly tossed it aside and forgotten about it?

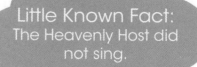

Little Known Fact: The Heavenly Host did not sing.

I urge you not to receive God's grace in vain. Now is the time of God's favor. Now is the time of His salvation. This is the best part of the birthday party. Your Heavenly Host gives His favor to you. Do not waste it.

LIFT

God, thank You for your favor. Thank You for giving me peace and salvation. Forgive me for times when I have abandoned Your favor. Remind me this Christmas of the words of Your Heavenly Host. Remind me that Your favor is on me. Help me to live my salvation to the fullest and to share Your favor with others. Amen.

LIVE

What is your favorite thing about birthday parties? What are some practical ways you can focus on celebrating Christ more this Christmas? Write a journal entry describing some new ways to celebrate Jesus' birth this year.

JOURNAL

December 14

LISTEN

A record of the genealogy of Jesus Christ the son of David, the son of Abraham: Abraham was the father of Isaac, Isaac the father of Jacob, Jacob the father of Judah and his brothers, Judah the father of Perez and Zerah, whose mother was Tamar, Perez the father of Hezron, Hezron the father of Ram, Ram the father of Amminadab, Amminadab the father of Nahshon, Nahshon the father of Salmon, Salmon the father of Boaz, whose mother was Rahab, Boaz the father of Obed, whose mother was Ruth, Obed the father of Jesse, and Jesse the father of King David. David was the father of

Solomon, whose mother had been Uriah's wife, Solomon the
father of Rehoboam, Rehoboam the father of Abijah, Abijah
the father of Asa, Asa the father of Jehoshaphat, Jehoshaphat
the father of Joram, Joram the father of Uzziah, Uzziah the
father of Jotham, Jotham the father of Ahaz, Ahaz the father
of Hezekiah, Hezekiah the father of Manasseh, Manasseh
the father of Amon, Amon the father of Josiah, and Josiah
the father of Jeconiah and his brothers at the time of the exile
to Babylon. After the exile to Babylon: Jeconiah was the father
of Shealtiel, Shealtiel the father of Zerubbabel, Zerubbabel
the father of Abiud, Abiud the father of Eliakim, Eliakim
the father of Azor, Azor the father of Zadok, Zadok the
father of Akim, Akim the father of Eliud, Eliud the father
of Eleazar, Eleazar the father of Matthan, Matthan the
father of Jacob, and Jacob the father of Joseph. The husband
of Mary, of whom was born Jesus, who is called Christ.

Matthew 1:1-16

LEARN

Reading the Christmas story each year has always been a great tradition for many families . Most of the time, we like to sit around the fire and read from Luke 2. That seems to be the most nostalgic version. It has that nice "Charlie Brown Christmas" feel to it. Besides, Mark and John skip over the Bethlehem account completely. And then there's Matthew, the tax collector. He begins his book very systematically, like any good accountant should. The first seventeen verses contain the family tree of Jesus. Now, genealogies normally don't get us too excited. We usually skip the genealogies. The reader doesn't want to butcher all those Hebrew names and embarrass himself (as you probably just did).

So it seems almost normal to skip to verse 18. And that's quite understandable because it's not your typical fireside reading. But every one of the names in Matthew 1 has a story behind it. Just like you and me, each of the people named has experienced the bitter repercussions of sin and the sweet feeling of grace. These are real people. They aren't made up. They aren't fictional characters in a fairy tale. They aren't from Harry Potter or the Hunger Games. They lived real lives at real times and in real places.

Little Known Fact: There are murderers, prostitutes, and rape victims in the family tree of Jesus.

Our Sovereign God guided and protected each family in this lineage whether it was faithful to Him or not. Many were not. Some were even wicked in the eyes of the Lord. There are murderers, prostitutes, and rape victims in the family tree of Jesus. And you thought your family was dysfunctional?

Each of these lives, these stories, stands on a timeline that began thousands of years ago with Father Abraham down to King David and ultimately down to Mary and Joseph and the Christ child.

The beautiful thing is that the family of Christ doesn't stop there. Just like Ruth, who was a Moabite and a Gentile, was allowed into the family tree, you and I are allowed to be a part of the family of God. We are a member of the beautiful line of David through our heritage in Jesus Christ.

97

Peter puts it this way, "But you are a chosen people, a royal priesthood, a holy nation, God's special possession, that you may declare the praises of him who called you out of darkness into his wonderful light. 1 Peter 2:9

See, you are part of the family of God. You are His prized possession.

Suddenly a genealogy is not so bad after all.

LIFT

Dear Father, this Christmas help me to draw close to my family. My family is not perfect mainly because I am not perfect. Let me be a living example of Jesus to those in my family who don't know Christ. Help us to set aside our differences and opinions and truly worship You this Christmas. And most of all, give our family peace this Christmas, the peace that passes all understanding. In Jesus' name, amen.

LIVE

Your family should be a major priority in your life. Take time to serve your immediate family this week. Write a journal entry and make a note of anyone in your family who doesn't know Christ. Write how you will minister to them this Christmas and make it a point to pray for them every day. If all of your family knows Christ, write down a prayer thanking Him for His goodness and for protecting your family with grace.

JOURNAL

December 15

Baby Talk

LISTEN

At that time Mary got ready and hurried to a town in the hill country of Judea, where she entered Zechariah's home and greeted Elizabeth. When Elizabeth heard Mary's greeting, the baby leaped in her womb, and Elizabeth was filled with the Holy Spirit. In a loud voice she exclaimed: "Blessed are you among women, and blessed is the child you will bear! But why am I so favored, that the mother of my Lord should come to me? As soon as the sound of your greeting reached my ears, the baby in my womb leaped for joy. Blessed is she who has believed that the Lord would fulfill his promises to her!"

Luke 1: 39-45

LEARN

Christmastime is my favorite time of year because Christmas means family is coming. Now, everyone likes to joke about relatives coming to stay at your house, but few things elicit more joy and happiness than being with family at Christmastime. Such is the occasion in the scripture you just read.

Mary, fresh off an angelic encounter, popped in on her cousin Elizabeth. Now, prior to this, Elizabeth had been in seclusion for about five months. Maybe she needed to rest. Watching my wife endure three pregnancies, I can assure you that a pregnant woman needs plenty of daily rest. Elizabeth, pregnant in her old age, probably needed the rest more than most. Maybe she was also a bit embarrassed. After all, her friends were all grandmothers, and she was preparing to have her firstborn. But my guess is that Elizabeth spent the better part of those five months in wonder over the fact that God had chosen her to be the mother of a special baby boy named John.

Elizabeth can be compared to Sarah of the Old Testament. Abraham's wife, too, was barren. If you recall, when God told her that she was going to have a son, Sarah laughed because she was very old. But after Isaac's birth, her laugh changed from a laugh of disbelief to a laugh of joy. It was in that moment of his birth that Sarah realized that God can do the impossible. I am going to submit to you that Elizabeth was probably thinking the same thing.

What Elizabeth could not have known was that the angel Gabriel had also made a visit to Mary's house. Remember, at the time, Mary was most certainly still a very young woman. Most scholars believe Mary was around 16 years old when she became pregnant with Jesus. And a very special thing happened when young Mary appeared at Elizabeth's door. Maybe it was the voice of Mary that the baby responded to. Luke says, "The baby leaped in Elizabeth's womb. And Elizabeth, filled with the Holy Spirit, proclaimed to Mary, 'Blessed are you among women and blessed is the fruit of your womb.'"

What a great moment. Mary came to share good news. Baby John was kicking up a storm in Elizabeth's womb, and Elizabeth received the blessing of the Holy Spirit in her life. I would say that was a great family visit! And to top it off, Elizabeth had the great distinction and honor of announcing the baby Jesus into this world.

We should never be surprised by the love of God. Our God is a god of surprises and a god of miracles. Elizabeth and Mary rejoiced at what God was doing in both their lives. I hope this Christmas season that you are rejoicing in what God is doing in your life. Be assured that God is at work this Christmas and that He wants to use you to accomplish His purpose when you least expect it.

Little Known Fact:
Most scholars believe Mary was around 16 years old when she became pregnant with Jesus.

103

LIFT

God I pray that You will use me this Christmas however You see fit. I will be open to Your leading and to Your direction. I know that You use the young and old alike. Help me to fulfill Your purposes in my generation. Thank You for sending Jesus to show me how to live out my days here on earth. I pray that each one is pleasing in Your sight. Amen.

LIVE

How is God at work in your life? Are you ready for your next assignment? Write a journal entry and list ways you are currently serving your family, your community, and your church. Are you letting God use you? Write out some goals for how you plan to use your gifts for God's Kingdom.

JOURNAL

December 16

Say It with Song

LISTEN

And Mary said: "My soul glorifies the Lord and my spirit rejoices in God my Savior, for he has been mindful of the humble state of his servant. From now on all generations will call me blessed, for the Mighty One has done great things for me – holy is his name. His mercy extends to those who fear him, from generation to generation. He has performed mighty deeds with his arm; he has scattered those who are proud in their inmost thoughts. He has brought down rulers from their thrones but has lifted up the humble. He has filled the hungry with good things but has sent the rich away empty. He has helped his servant Israel, remembering to be merciful to Abraham and his descendants forever, even as he said to our fathers."

Luke 1:46-55

LEARN

Christmas is a fantastic time of year because everywhere you go there are reminders of Jesus. Decorations abound. People smile and say, "Merry Christmas." Nativity scenes are displayed.

My excitement really begins to grow around the week of Thanksgiving when radio stations start to play Christmas songs. I love that, during the month of December, I get to hear songs about Jesus in department stores, restaurants, and coffee shops.

I love Christmas carols. My favorite all-time Christmas song is "Walking in a Winter Wonderland." I sing it all year long because it reminds me of the joy of Christmas. I have noticed that people don't seem to appreciate it as much in July, but who cares? They look at me like I am crazy when I burst into song and say, "Now everyone sing along." I have never understood why some of the greatest songs ever written are only sung for one month out of the year.

Songs have an important and rather dramatic role in the celebration of Christmas. Our Christmas carols carry with them the full spectrum of human emotion. They magically capture the wide range of emotion that each Christmas carries with it. From the anticipation found in "Santa Clause Is Coming to Town" to the worship and reverence within "Silent Night," we express our emotions in song each Christmas.

Mary, the mother of Jesus, wrote the very first Christmas song. Mary's song was filled with the emotion of Christmas. She began by praising God for who He is and for what He was going to do. Her song is filled with anticipation. Mary believed what the angel told her and what was confirmed to her through her visit to Elizabeth. In Luke 1:45, Elizabeth says to Mary, "Blessed is she who has believed that what the Lord has said to her will be accomplished!" Mary was blessed because of her belief, and her song proclaimed that belief in worship.

Mary's song also revealed her excitement. She was excited to be a part of God's plan and to be chosen. Much was still unknown to her, but nonetheless she was filled with hope. Mary was needed and had found God's grand purpose for her life.

Little Known Fact:
Mary, the mother of Jesus, wrote the very first Christmas song.

Mary was thankful and confident in God. She thanked Him in advance for what He would do and declared her confidence in her Lord. Mary's song is a wonderful reminder of what our Christmas songs are really about.

When you sing this Christmas, pay attention to the emotions expressed in the song, and take advantage of every opportunity to worship. Enjoy the anticipation and excitement of Christmas. Be thankful and confident in God's enduring plan. Renew your commitment to your role within the Kingdom.

In Ephesians 5 we are told to "Sing and make music in your heart to the Lord, always giving thanks to God the Father for everything in the name of our Lord Jesus Christ." Enjoy the songs of Christmas, and remember, you do not have to put away your Christmas music on December 26th.

LIFT

Lord, I thank You for the emotions that Christmas brings. Thank You for the opportunity to sing and to worship this Christmas. Help me to be confident in You and to renew my commitment to serving You. Restore to me the joy and anticipation of Christmas. Please make this Christmas full of worship because You truly are worthy of my praise.

LIVE

What is your favorite Christmas song? What emotions does the song evoke? Write a journal entry about all of the emotions you experience at Christmas. How can those emotions point you towards a worshipful response to Christ's birth?

JOURNAL

December 17

Let It Be

LISTEN

"I am the Lord's servant," Mary answered. "May your word to me be fulfilled."

Luke 1:38

But Mary treasured up all these things and pondered them in her heart.

Luke 2:19

LEARN

I was called to ministry in the summer of 1984. It wasn't audible, and honestly, it wasn't all that joyful. Don't get me wrong. There was excitement, but I was fearful. Ministry? Me? I had trouble putting two sentences together. I was scared to death to speak in front of people, and I had (and still have) an ADD problem. Sounds like "Pastor of the Year" material, right?

But I did one thing right that summer. I said yes.

And the rest, as they say, is history. Not all of it has been perfect. In fact, most of it hasn't been. But I did the one thing many people never get around to doing. I told God I would go wherever He leads me. I told Him I would serve Him for better or for worse, in good times and in bad times.

Now my response was not as brave or noble as the one you just read from our friend Mary. When asked to carry the Christ child in her womb, she said, "I am your servant, may your word to me be fulfilled." One translation says, "May it be as you have said."

I love what the Message paraphrase says:

"Yes, I see it all now: I'm the Lord's maid, ready to serve. Let it be with me just as you say."

Really? There is actually a passage in the Bible that calls the Virgin Mary a maid? It seems a bit irreverent, doesn't it? I think it really captures just what an amazing servant the mother of our Lord really was. She was a servant of the Most High God.

She was willing to serve her God in whatever capacity asked of her. She was willing to sacrifice her reputation and her future to advance the Kingdom of God.

It's astounding to me that Mary's two responses to the Angel delivering the messianic news were, "How will this be?" and "Let it be."

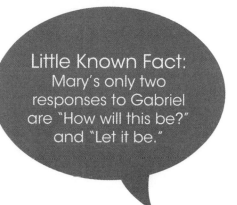

Little Known Fact: Mary's only two responses to Gabriel are "How will this be?" and "Let it be."

Have you ever said that to God when He nudged you with a divine assignment? "Lord, let it be as you have said."

One of the reasons I love Mary is that I can relate to her. She too was called. She too felt inadequate and unworthy. She too wondered why God was calling her for such a time as this. But Mary said the one word that is sometimes hard to say when God is calling you to big works in His Kingdom.

She said yes.

I don't know your story. I don't know what stirs your heart. But do this for me, friend. If God is calling you, if He has a divine assignment, if He is looking your way to accomplish His work, if He needs a helping hand...

Say yes.

LIFT

God, my declaration to You today is whatever You prompt me to do, whatever your Spirit tells me or urges me to do—my answer in advance is yes," even if it stretches me to the limit of my faith. Teach me to say yes more often when it comes to being a Christ follower. I just want to thank You today for Mary. I am thankful that when You called her, she made herself completely available to You. Lord, use me for Your Kingdom this Christmas. I want to use my gifts to help others find Jesus. Please have Your way in my life. Let it be, dear Lord. Let it be. Amen.

LIVE

The cost of being a fully-devoted follower of Jesus is great. What are the things that keep you from following Jesus and being obedient to His call? Write a journal entry and rate yourself on a scale of 1-10 in terms of your dedication to the cause of Christ. What areas of your life do you need to pray about in order to be more obedient to Jesus?

JOURNAL

December 18

LISTEN

And Jacob the father of Joseph, the husband of Mary, of whom was born Jesus, who was called Christ.

Matthew 1:16

When Joseph woke up, he did what the angel of the Lord had commanded him and took Mary home as his wife. But he did not consummate their marriage until she gave birth to a son. And he gave him the name Jesus.

Matthew 1:24-25

LEARN

One of the reasons I love the Bible is that there are so many mentors that I can learn from and emulate. Take Joseph for instance. Joseph, the earthly father of Jesus, appears to be an exceptionally good man. I only wish we knew more about him. In my humble opinion, Joseph didn't get enough press time in the Bible. Did you know that Mark, John, and Paul never even mention Joseph in their writings? C'mon, boys, where's the love? But even when he does get mentioned in scripture, it almost feels a bit backhanded. I have to chuckle at the way Matthew describes him in the genealogy verse (Matthew 1:16). Joseph is known in the Bible as "the husband of Mary." Really? That's what Joseph gets in the family memoirs? It makes me wonder what his construction buddies would have said to Joseph had they been able to read that! "Hey, Joe, what's up? Or should I say, " How's Mary's husband"? (Cue cheesy laugh here.) That kind of sums up the life of this simple carpenter from Nazareth.

But I love studying Joseph. He was a lot like you and me. The Bible certainly implies that Joseph was a steady man of character. The New Living Translation says in Matthew 1:19 that he was a "good man." He was full of integrity, and he loved the Lord with all of his heart. I would submit to you that Joseph probably didn't mind being called the "husband of Mary." I doubt status was important to him. A man of his character just doesn't dwell on those kinds of things.

Joseph also was a man of commitment. He was head-over-heels in love with his teenage sweetheart, Mary. We read in Matthew 1:18 that Joseph was pledged to be married, or betrothed, to Mary. Don't underestimate that level of commitment. It was a serious covenant between a man and a woman. It was like saying, "I am prepared to spend the remainder of my days with you and you only until death do us part."

Another thing I love about Joseph is that he was morally pure. He, too, had saved himself for marriage. He, too, was committed to being a virgin until the marriage covenant was sealed.

Think about the world we live in. The thought that both parties would save themselves for marriage is so old fashioned. In some circles it's considered foolish. But God honors this beautiful expression of sexual purity. My guess is that Joseph never put any pressure on Mary. He wanted them both to remain pure until they were married.

What about the ultimate test…the announcement? It must have been devastating to hear that Mary was pregnant. We forget how young they both were. Most young couples would have bailed out and buckled under the pressure. But Joseph handled it with humility and grace . Remember Matthew 1:19? "Because Joseph was a righteous man, and did not want to expose Mary to public disgrace, he had in mind to divorce her quietly." This must have absolutely split Joseph's heart in two. His reputation in the community was undoubtedly tarnished. It was an embarrassing development, to say the least. Yet Joseph, the father of Jesus, remains steadfast toward the goal. He draws strength from his faith in God, and God faithfully uses him to accomplish this enormous, divine task.

Matthew 1:24-25 is a good way to finish this brief look at Joseph. "When Joseph woke up, he did what the angel of the Lord had commanded him and took Mary home as his wife.

But he did not consummate their marriage until she gave birth to a son. And he gave him the name Jesus."

Joseph did what the Lord commanded. He obeyed the Lord in all things. He obeyed when it was not easy to be obedient. He finished his assignment.

We don't hear much about Joseph after the birth of Jesus, but this man from Nazareth, the earthly father of Jesus, was a really good man, and you would be wise to emulate his life.

Little Known Fact:
Mark, John, and Paul never even mention Joseph in their writings.

122

LIFT

Jesus, thank You for men of faith like Joseph who are men of integrity, men of commitment, and men of purity. I hope that I can live out the scriptures much like Your earthly father lived out the scriptures. And I want to pause right now and thank You for my earthly father. May Your blessing be on him right now whether he is in heaven or here on earth. I pray all these things in the sweet name of Jesus. Amen.

LIVE

This reading today probably felt like it was intended for men only. But all of us can take a lesson from the life of Joseph. Virtues like character and integrity are the foundation of our Christian faith. Write a journal entry and describe an earthly mentor that you have encountered who has exhibited some of the same virtues as Joseph. Make it a goal in your journaling to write down some areas that you must sharpen in order to be a man or woman after God's heart.

JOURNAL

December 19

Check It Out

LISTEN

When the angels had left them and gone into heaven, the shepherds said to one another, "Let's go to Bethlehem and see this thing that has happened, which the Lord has told us about."

So they hurried off and found Mary and Joseph, and the baby, who was lying in the manger. When they had seen him, they spread the word concerning what had been told them about this child, and all who heard it were amazed at what the shepherds said to them. But Mary treasured up all these things and pondered them in her heart. The shepherds returned, glorifying and praising God for all the things they had heard and seen, which were just as they had been told.

Luke 2:15-20

LEARN

Has anybody ever told you about something that sounded so wonderful you just had to experience it for yourself? Maybe they recommended a great book, a fantastic movie, a delicious restaurant, or an amazing vacation destination? I know that, when I hear people I love and respect speaking of things that they find enjoyable or beneficial, I want to experience those things as well. There is often a buzz surrounding great things. People talk about them and the legend grows. There is no greater publicity than word-of-mouth advertising!

The birth of Jesus created a bit of a buzz. The angels announced His birth to the shepherds, the Heavenly Host testified to the wonder of the Christ child, and then the shepherds went to see it for themselves. It all sounded so wonderful that they had to experience it with their own eyes. When the angels left, the shepherds' immediate response was to say, "Let's go check it out." Then they hurried off to visit Mary, Joseph, and the baby.

The fact that the shepherds left their flocks to go and see the Christ child is no minor detail. Shepherds do not just leave their sheep. Shepherds love their sheep. They protect their sheep. Their sheep must be taken care of to protect the livelihood of the shepherd.

Have you ever wondered why God chose to reveal the birth of His Son to shepherds before kings, religious leaders, and those with financial power? God does have a soft spot for shepherds and a track record of using them. Abraham, Moses, and David were shepherds. Jesus would even refer to Himself as the "Good Shepherd."

Shepherds were probably the best-equipped people to comprehend that a baby in a manger was the messiah. They didn't scoff at the simplicity or doubt because their expectations were not met. They just went to see it for themselves.

What they saw was probably not all that spectacular. There was a newborn baby in a manger. He wasn't glowing. There was no halo over His head. There were no diamond-encrusted pacifiers or extravagances of any kind. There was a very young and tired mother. There was a concerned and protective father. There just wasn't much else to see.

I imagine that the shepherds recounted to Mary and Joseph the words the angel had spoken to them and that in turn Mary and Joseph shared of their angelic encounters. They probably had much to talk about as they gazed into the infant eyes of the promised king. They must have wondered how this child would grow and what events would unfold throughout His life. We have no record of their conversation, but one thing is clear...the shepherds' visit sparked their hope that the Messiah had finally come.

Little Known Fact: God has a soft spot for shepherds. Abraham, Moses, and David were all shepherds.

At this point Jesus had performed no miracles. He had healed no one. He had not preached a sermon or even uttered a word. Jesus was just a baby lying in a manger. After the shepherds had seen Him though, they spread the word concerning this child. They passed on what they had experienced, and everyone who heard their testimony was amazed.

The shepherds testified to their hope, but we have something more. We have Christ crucified. We have the resurrection. We have the Holy Spirit. We have salvation. Now we must testify to what we have seen and heard. We must share our experience with others.

This Christmas, check Jesus out for yourself. Experience Him firsthand. Then share your experience with others, so they can see Him too.

LIFT

Lord, I thank You for allowing me to experience You firsthand. Help me to be aware of Your presence this Christmas, and make my visits with You sweet. Give me courage to share You with others. I pray that everyone I know will know You too.

LIVE

Have you experienced Jesus for yourself? Write a journal entry describing what you have seen and heard about Jesus. How can you help create a buzz about Jesus this Christmas?

JOURNAL

December 20

Starstruck

LISTEN

After Jesus was born in Bethlehem in Judea, during the time of King Herod, Magi from the east came to Jerusalem and asked, "Where is the one who has been born king of the Jews? We saw his star when it rose and have come to worship him."

Matthew 2:1-2

When they saw the star, they were overjoyed. On coming to the house, they saw the child with his mother Mary, and they bowed down and worshiped him. Then they opened their treasures and presented him with gifts of gold, frankincense, and myrrh.

Matthew 2:10-11

LEARN

Have you ever met someone famous? It seems like the few times I have met someone famous, I was caught completely off guard. I was either unprepared, didn't know what to say, or had no idea who I was talking to.

I met former President George W. Bush once. It was in the mid 1990s when he was part owner of the Texas Rangers and was running for Governor of Texas. He pulled up next to me at a stoplight and rolled down his window to have a conversation. We chatted throughout the red light about baseball, the NBA finals, and the weather. There were several other people in the car with me, but none of them said a word. When he drove off, I asked if anybody knew who that guy was and that's when I saw the "Bush for Governor" sticker on the back of his car. My friends all laughed at me for having no idea who I was talking to. It's probably a good thing that I didn't recognize him, because if I had, I probably would have been starstruck .

The Magi in the Christmas story are different from me. They were waiting for the Messiah to be born, and they were starstruck in a different fashion. They were watching for a specific star to appear, and when God placed that star in the sky to announce the birth of Jesus, the Magi took off to find the Christ child. They followed the star until they found Jesus.

The Magi were powerful and wealthy. They probably created quite a stir when they came into town. We do not know how many Magi there were. The common idea that there were three comes from the number of gifts that they brought. The number was probably larger and they would have traveled with a massive entourage. When the Magi showed up, people noticed.

King Herod certainly noticed, and he was not happy. The Magi searched for Jesus to worship Him and to lend their support to His Kingdom. They came prepared with traditional gifts of royalty. They brought anointing oil called myrrh, perfume called frankincense, and valuables of gold.

When they found Jesus, they knew exactly what to do. They welcomed and worshiped the King of Kings .

What about you? Are you ready to encounter Jesus this Christmas? Do you understand who He is and what He desires for you?

As you encounter Jesus this Christmas, you do not need to be starstruck. He loves you and wants you to know Him intimately. Search for Jesus, and you will find Him.

But what about a gift?

Christmas is all about gifts. God gave His Son to the world. The Magi traveled from afar to bring gifts to the newly born king.

Little Known Fact:
We do not know how many Magi there were. The common idea that there were three comes from the number of gifts that they brought.

I think that the Magi had the right idea. Wouldn't you like to give God a gift this Christmas? Have you ever wondered what He would want? What could we possible give the Almighty God?

There really is only one answer. We give Him our lives. That is what God desires. Our perfect gift to God is a surrendered heart and an obedient life. Go ahead and splurge this Christmas and give yourself completely to God.

LIFT

God, thank You for sending Your Son in the form of a man. I praise You for becoming like me, so I can know You. Help me to approach You boldly this Christmas and make Yourself known to me in greater ways. I offer You my life this Christmas. It is the only gift You want, and it is all I have to offer.

LIVE

Do you ever find yourself starstruck when spending time with Jesus? Why or why not? Write a journal entry about the things that make Jesus amazing and the things that make Him accessible. Is there a part of your life that you have held back from Jesus? If so, use this opportunity to give yourself completely to Him.

JOURNAL

December 21

Dear Herod

LISTEN

After Jesus was born in Bethlehem in Judea, during the time of King Herod, Magi from the east came to Jerusalem and asked, "Where is the one who has been born king of the Jews? We saw his star when it rose and have come to worship him." When King Herod heard this he was disturbed, and all Jerusalem with him. When he had called together all the people's chief priests and teachers of the law, he asked them where the Messiah was to be born. "In Bethlehem in Judea," they replied, "for this is what the prophet has written:
"'But you, Bethlehem, in the land of Judah, are by no means least among the rulers of Judah; for out of you will come a ruler who will shepherd my people Israel.'"

Then Herod called the Magi secretly and found out from them the exact time the star had appeared. He sent them to Bethlehem and said, "Go and search carefully for the child. As soon as you find him, report to me, so that I too may go and worship him."

After they had heard the king, they went on their way, and the star they had seen when it rose went ahead of them until it stopped over the place where the child was. When they saw the star, they were overjoyed. On coming to the house, they saw the child with his mother Mary, and they bowed down and worshiped him. Then they opened their treasures and presented him with gifts of gold, frankincense and myrrh. And having been warned in a dream not to go back to Herod, they returned to their country by another route.

Matthew 2:1-12

LEARN

An open letter to Herod the Great:

Dear King,

I only call you that out of respect for the office. My parents taught me at a very young age to respect leaders no matter how I perceive them. So I'll stick with addressing you as king although my true allegiance is to Jesus of Nazareth.

I'm writing you to share my thoughts on how you handled the whole "Bethlehem Experience." My guess is that you aren't interested in my opinion, but I felt compelled to write anyway. Like you, I am a leader, and I often receive letters from critics that I'd just as soon toss in the trash. However, more often than not, I find that there is usually some good advice sprinkled into the criticism. I've always thought that how a man handles criticism goes a long way in determining his true character.

First, I'll focus on the positives. The temple you built is magnificent and most impressive. I especially like the Western Wall, as there's something very holy about it. Again, well done, my friend. I have a hunch people will be talking about your temple for thousands of years. Also, thanks for your contributions to the water supplies in Jerusalem. Fresh water is important, and I am sure the people of Jerusalem will be much healthier in the long run drinking clean water. By the way—a quick thought—you should bottle the water and sell it down at the city market. You could make some serious denarii, bro (my two mites' worth).

My first question is why are you threatened by a baby? This little boy just wants a chance to grow up like any other boy. I mean, I get it that He's special, but why not give Him a chance? What if He really is the Son of God? What better ally for your kingship? Can I be honest, friend? The decree you issued to slaughter all the baby boys ages two and under just absolutely broke my heart. You were a baby once. Those boys were born to be leaders in their families. They were future husbands and future fathers and grandfathers. As a leader, you need to have sensitivity for the sanctity of life. My prayer is that you will think twice before making such a tragic decision again.

My second question is merely my advice from a public relations standpoint. Why do you treat your family so poorly? I have heard rumors that you actually executed members of your own family including some of your children and your beautiful wife! My dear King, tell me it isn't true! Imagine the PR nightmare when the cover of the Jerusalem News reads, "Herod the Great Executes His Lovely Wife Mariamne." Brother, I think you know this isn't going to bode well with potential voters.

One final question. Why did you deceive the Magi into thinking that you were going to actually worship the Christ child? We both know you had no intention of worshipping Jesus. You merely were trying to eliminate Him so that He would not become more powerful than you. Here's the problem, my King. He is more powerful than you. He doesn't need a palatial estate or a golden throne or even a jewel-encrusted crown. Let me tell you about my King Jesus. He may have been born in a barn, and his first bed was a feeding trough. These facts I cannot dispute. But God is going to exalt this son of a carpenter someday and He, not you, will be the King of Kings and the Lord of Lords.

In closing, what breaks my heart the most is that the one person that could have brought peace into this distressed life that we are living was the very person that you tried to kill. You were the voice of opposition when you could have been the voice of recognition. And I am praying that you will change your heart about Jesus. That you could see Him as I see Him. That you wouldn't miss Christmas again like you did that silent night in Bethlehem.

Little Known Fact: Herod the Great executed his wife Mariamne.

This letter has gone too long, and for that I am sorry. Herod, think this over because here is the good news. It's not too late. Jesus will never grow tired of extending His Grace to you. He loves you and longs for you to repent. His love is like an ocean. It is never-ending and flows freely. My prayer is that one day you will humble yourself and bow the knee and confess Jesus Christ as Lord.

With the utmost respect,

LIFT

Lord, I humbly bow before Your Son Jesus. He is the King of Kings and the Lord of Lords. Help me to never be obsessed with my will, my needs, or my agenda. You are my obsession Jesus. You are my Rock and my Redeemer. And I worship You this Christmas. I love you, Jesus. Amen

LIVE

Hopefully you found our letter to Herod helpful. It's hard to understand why he did the things that he did. But before you cast the first stone, think about your own life. How many times have you missed Christmas entirely? How many times have you made Christmas all about you? In the journal entry write a letter to Jesus and thank Him for His grace and His mercy. Tell Him how you are going to shine His light this Christmas.

JOURNAL

December 22

A Voice of Recognition

LISTEN

Now there was a man in Jerusalem called Simeon, who was righteous and devout. He was waiting for the consolation of Israel, and the Holy Spirit was on him. It had been revealed to him by the Holy Spirit that he would not die before he had seen the Lord's Messiah. Moved by the Spirit, he went into the temple courts. When the parents brought in the child Jesus to do for him what the custom of the Law required, Simeon took him in his arms and praised God, saying:
"Sovereign Lord, as you have promised, you may now dismiss your servant in peace. For my eyes have seen your salvation, which you have prepared in the sight of all nations: a light for revelation to the Gentiles, and the glory of your people Israel."
The child's father and mother marveled at what was said

about him. Then Simeon blessed them and said to Mary, his mother: "This child is destined to cause the falling and rising of many in Israel, and to be a sign that will be spoken against, so that the thoughts of many hearts will be revealed. And a sword will pierce your own soul too."

Luke 2:25-35

LEARN

Most people love babies. Have you ever noticed how people light up when a mom walks into a room with a newborn baby in her arms? People gravitate toward the baby. They want to talk to the baby, touch the baby, hold the baby, kiss the baby, pinch the baby's cheeks, smell the baby…

I don't get it. Don't get me wrong. I am not anti-baby, but I prefer to keep them at a healthy distance. I am aware that my feelings on babies are a bit unpopular, but the truth of the matter is that babies kind of freak me out.

There is a lot of risk involved in baby interactions.

For instance, you can never tell if the baby is a boy or girl and you run the risk of offending the parents if you call a he a she or a she a he. I can't tell you how many times I have said, "Oh, she's beautiful" only to have the mom snap back with "He's a boy!" Well, ma'am, do us all a favor and take the pink jumper off of that boy and cover him up in something blue.

I'm scared to death to hold another person's baby. Babies squirm, and I just can't handle that kind of responsibility. I have enough pressure in my life and don't need the added weight of keeping someone else's baby alive while holding it. I know me.

I have dropped things before…valuable things…and broken them.

Then there is the grossness factor. Babies do things that I don't want any part of. Diapers leak. Blowouts occur. Spit-up comes without warning. If you get any of that stuff on your clothes, the smell is not coming out.

So, surely you can understand my reluctance when people walk up to me and hand me their baby. People do this to me because I am a pastor. They want me to hold their baby, share in their joy, and say a blessing over the child. Even though I have what I consider to be a healthy fear of babies, I never forget what an honor it is to behold new life and ask for God's blessing.

Jesus was forty days old when Mary and Joseph took Him to Jerusalem to present Him to the Lord. A righteous man named Simeon was moved by the Spirit of the Lord to go the temple. The Holy Spirit had revealed to Simeon that he would not die until he had seen the promised Messiah. When Simeon encountered Jesus, he took the infant in his arms and he praised God because he knew that he was holding the Messiah.

Little Known Fact: Jesus was forty days old when Mary and Joseph took Him to Jerusalem to present Him to the Lord.

Simeon prophesied about what Jesus would do. He blessed the family and spoke powerful words about their newborn son. I imagine that the words God spoke through Simeon that day echoed often in Mary's mind. Here was yet another confirmation of who this child would be.

Simeon's life was complete because he had seen the Savior. I assure you that your life will never be complete until you recognize who Jesus is. When you hold onto Jesus as your Savior, you are prepared to face eternity.

Make it a point to truly behold Jesus this Christmas. Recognize who Jesus is. Consider the ramifications of His life, death, and resurrection. Hold Him close and never let Him go.

LIFT

Lord, help me this Christmas to see Jesus as much more than just a baby. Remind me of everything You did through Your Son. Help me to cling to Jesus and to fully grasp the reality of His life, death, and resurrection. Make my life complete by helping me to hold fast to Jesus.

LIVE

When you consider Jesus, what stands out the most to you regarding His life on earth? How does intentionally thinking about Jesus change your perspective on life? Write a journal entry about how your life is complete because of knowing Jesus.

JOURNAL

December 23

Anna and Sophia

LISTEN

There was also a prophet, Anna, the daughter of Penuel, of the tribe of Asher. She was very old; she had lived with her husband seven years after her marriage, and then was a widow until she was eighty-four. She never left the temple but worshiped night and day, fasting and praying. Coming up to them at that very moment, she gave thanks to God and spoke about the child to all who were looking forward to the redemption of Jerusalem.

When Joseph and Mary had done everything required by the Law of the Lord, they returned to Galilee to their own town of Nazareth. And the child grew and became strong; he was filled with wisdom, and the grace of God was on him.

Luke 2:36-40

LEARN

I wish you could have known my great grandmother Sophia. She was born and raised in Vergennes, Illinois, just a stone's throw from Du Quoin where they have the Illinois State Fair. She was the daughter of a German immigrant whose family settled in the Midwest in the mid 1800s. She outlived her husband by almost 40 years and worked each day diligently in her garden until she was one-hundred years old. She was a skilled seamstress, an incredible cook, an avid canner, and made the best strawberry-rhubarb pie you have ever tasted. Grandma was also the hospitable landlady to over 100 wild turkeys in the massive oak tree that stood next to her 130-year-old house. I use that word hospitable loosely, for every November, around the 4th Thursday, one of those turkeys gave its life for the sake of culinary excellence.

But the most vivid memory I have of Grandmother Sophia is one of her kneeling bedside on the old hard-wood floor in prayer. She would rise early in the morning to talk to her Redeemer. She actually said most of her prayers in German, and I couldn't tell you much about what she said, but I can tell you that I have never heard anyone pray like that before. Her heart was so gentle. Her words were so tender. Her disposition was so humble. Her wisdom was so evident.

My grandmother lived to be 103 years old, and she lived every day for Jesus Christ. And I share this family testimony because she reminds me of the prophet Anna who is mentioned briefly at the end of Luke 2. What a wonderful woman of God. She was a woman living in a man's world. Women rarely spoke in public, let alone exhibited leadership. But Anna, the daughter of Penuel, of the tribe of Asher, was a woman of great virtue and a woman after God's heart. Scripture says that "she never left the temple but worshiped night and day, fasting and praying." Anna literally lived in the temple.

Do you ever read words like that and feel a little spiritually lazy? I do. In fact, when I read about this woman, I stopped reading and writing long enough to ask God to make me a little more like Anna and a little less like me. To help me to be the kind of Christ-follower who will fast without announcing it, who will worship like no one is watching.

Well, Anna had a small but important role with the baby Jesus. Mary and Joseph had taken their baby boy to the temple to be presented for consecration and to offer a sacrifice. After Jesus receives a wonderful blessing from Simeon, Anna came up to be a voice of thanksgiving and praise, as she gave thanks to God for sending Jesus to be the redeemer of the whole world. Her blessings and prophetic words provided a very special moment for young Mary and Joseph .

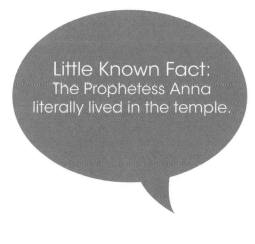

Little Known Fact:
The Prophetess Anna literally lived in the temple.

Grandma Sophia lived to be 103 before she died in her sleep and went to be with the Lord. I love remembering her sweet spirit and her devotion to her heavenly father. She prayed without ceasing and loved with no conditions. She was my version of Anna. And I will never forget her.

LIFT

Lord, in the midst of all the hustle and bustle of Christmas, I pause to give thanks for women like Anna. She was a woman after God's heart. I pray that I too have a desire to worship You 24/7. That I would commit my days to prayer and personal worship and that You would be honored and praised. Unto You be all glory, honor, and power, oh, Lord. Amen.

LIVE

Maybe you read this chapter and felt like it was primarily for women. But Anna is a mentor to all of us. Her diligence in prayer, discipline when fasting, and her passion for Jesus are all virtues and actions to emulate. Write a journal entry and make a plan for a daily quiet time for the upcoming new year. Tell God how you plan to personally worship Him each day. Then keep the commitment!

JOURNAL

December 24

LISTEN

"But what about you?" he asked. "Who do you say I am?"
Simon Peter answered, "You are the Christ, the Son of the
living God."

Matthew 16:15-16

LEARN

It is December 24th…Christmas Eve.

This day means many different things to many different people.

For some, the day will be filled with activity, preparations, and stress.

For others, the day will hold loneliness, disappointment, and despair.

For many, the day will bring anticipation, hope, and joy.

For just about everyone, the day will bring questions.

Did I fix enough food? What am I going to wear? What could possibly be in this package? What time is church? How am I going to pay for all of this? Do I really have to wear this sweater? Why can't you kids get along with one another? Why does everyone leave when I stand under the mistletoe?

During this Advent season, you have read what 23 voices had to say about Jesus. I hope that you have paid close attention to the wisdom revealed through each of those voices. I pray that your relationship with Jesus is stronger today because He is speaking to you.

You know what others have said about Jesus, but what about you? What does your voice say about Jesus?

We all have questions, but did you know that Jesus has

questions too? This Christmas, He wants to hear your voice.

The question Jesus asked His disciples in Matthew 16 is the most important question we are faced with this Christmas.

"But what about you?" He asked. "Who do you say that I am?"

Peter's response was perfect. He said, "You are the Christ, the Son of the Living God."

Jesus' question demands an answer. Not answering is not an option. In Philippians 2:11 we are told that one day every knee will bow and every tongue will confess that Jesus Christ is Lord. We all must give an answer.

Who do you say Jesus is?

Little Known Fact:
The Hebrew name for
Jesus is Yeshua.

LIFT

God, thank You for sending Your Son. Thank You for revealing to me who He is. Thank You for the many voices that testify, "Jesus is the Christ, the Son of the Living God." Help my life make that declaration every day.

LIVE

This is your opportunity to add your voice to the mix. Who do you say Jesus is? Write a journal entry answering Jesus' question, "Who do you say that I am?"

JOURNAL

December 25

The Voice of
God

LISTEN

He says, "Be still, and know that I am God; I will be exalted among the nations, I will be exalted in the earth."

The Lord Almighty is with us; the God of Jacob is our fortress.

Psalm 46:10-11

165

LEARN

I have the good fortune of writing this Christmas Day chapter while gazing at snow-capped mountains that are fixed against the bluest sky I have ever laid eyes on. There is a slight breeze blowing through the mountainside, and although the temperature is chilly, there happens to be a burst of warm sunshine welcoming my skin. My task is to write the final chapter entitled "The Voice of God," but the only two words that come to mind are these:

Be still.

Just be still.

Christmas mornings are amazing, aren't they? I can just about imagine what you might be up to today. Perhaps there's already chaos. Maybe you've been up for hours making sure that everything is ready. Gifts have been purchased. Food has been cooked. Stockings are filled. Credit cards are maxed.

Christmas Day is here.

Will you take time to hear the voice of God? Will you pause for a moment and soak in the grandeur of it all?

Can I impart some Christmas Day wisdom?

Be still.

Be still and thank Him for His mercies that are new this Christmas Day.

Be still and ponder His amazing grace and His loving compassion.

Be still and let the Spirit of the Living God wash over you.

Little Known Fact: The author of Psalm 46 is unknown.

Be still and grateful for the earthly family God has given you.

Be still and fathom His immeasurable love.

Be still and mediate on the salvation given to you.

Be still and adore the baby Jesus in a manger.

Be still and see Him on the old rugged cross.

Be still as you envision the empty tomb.

Be still and know that He is God.

Be still.

Just be still this Christmas Day.

And listen to the voice of God.......

LIFT

Lord, on this Christmas Day, I ask that You help me to be still and know that You are God. And ready my heart to tell someone about the love of Jesus this Christmas.

LIVE

No Journal entry today. Just be still. And when you are out and about today, be quick to listen and slow to speak. Find those who need the love of Jesus and minister to them. Listen to their stories and pray with them .